# Rita Moreno

## A Little Golden Book® Biography

By Maria Correa

Ilustrated by Maine Diaz

🌹 A GOLDEN BOOK • NEW YORK

Text copyright © 2023 by Maria Correa
Cover art and interior illustrations copyright © 2023 by Maine Diaz
All rights reserved. Published in the United States by Golden Books, an imprint of Random House Children's Books, a division of Penguin Random House LLC, 1745 Broadway, New York, NY 10019. Golden Books, A Golden Book, A Little Golden Book, the G colophon, and the distinctive gold spine are registered trademarks of Penguin Random House LLC.
rhcbooks.com
Educators and librarians, for a variety of teaching tools, visit us at RHTeachersLibrarians.com
Library of Congress Control Number: 2022942320
ISBN 978-0-593-64514-7 (trade) — ISBN 978-0-593-64515-4 (ebook)
Printed in the United States of America
10 9 8 7 6 5 4 3 2 1

Rosa Dolores Alverío was born on December 11, 1931, on the island of Puerto Rico. Known as Rosita, she grew up in Juncos (HOON-kos), a small town near a magnificent rain forest called El Yunque (JUNE-ke). There, she lived in a pink house with her mother, Rosa María, her father, Paco, and her little brother, Francisco.

Rosita loved Puerto Rico. She loved its colorful flowers, its sweet fruit, and its whistling frogs called coquíes (ko-KEE-es). She loved running barefoot and splashing in the nearby stream while her mother washed clothes and shared stories with the other Juncos women.

When Rosita was five years old, her mother decided to leave Puerto Rico. They boarded a ship that would take them from the home they had always known to a new life in New York City.

Rosita saw the Statue of Liberty for the first time and thought its torch looked like a giant ice cream cone.

At first, Rosita didn't like New York City. She missed her old life. But things got better when she started taking Spanish dance lessons. Her teacher, Paco Cansino, was the uncle and teacher of the famous actor Rita Hayworth.

When Rosita was thirteen, she acted in her first Broadway play, called *Skydrift*. She loved it so much that, when she was sixteen, she quit school to focus on becoming a performer. Her mother brought her to the famous Waldorf Astoria hotel to meet the head of MGM Studios. He hired Rosita then and there, and she and Rosa María moved to California to live near the studios where movies were made.

Rosita's first film role was in the movie *So Young, So Bad*, in which she played a troubled teen. It is her only credit as Rosita. From then on, she was known as Rita Moreno.

Although Rita was a talented actor, she was often typecast, or given the same types of roles, because of her appearance. These characters from various cultures were not always well written and didn't give Rita a chance to fully showcase her skills.

Then, in 1952, Rita was given an exciting part in the musical film *Singin' in the Rain*. She played the glamorous movie star, Zelda Zanders. *Singin' in the Rain* remains one of the most famous Hollywood musicals of all time.

In 1961, Rita landed her biggest role yet: Anita, in the film adaptation of the Broadway musical *West Side Story*. Anita was a Puerto Rican living in New York City. Outspoken and full of life, she felt like a character Rita was born to play.

She rehearsed day and night to learn the complicated dance routines. Her hard work would soon be rewarded. . . .

Rita won an Oscar, an award given for excellence in film, for her outstanding performance as Anita in *West Side Story*. Because she didn't expect to win, she hadn't prepared a speech. All she could think to say was, "I can't believe it!"

That day, Rita became the first Latina to win an Oscar. People living in Rita's old neighborhood in New York City were thrilled to see someone from Puerto Rico on that stage. They opened their windows and shouted, "¡Ganó! She won!"

Surprisingly, after *West Side Story*, Rita continued to be offered small roles. She turned them down and took a break from acting. Instead, she spent her time fighting for social causes she believed in, like equal rights for women and Black Americans.

In 1963, Rita attended the March on Washington and was in the crowd by the Lincoln Memorial when Reverend Martin Luther King Jr. made his iconic "I Have a Dream" speech.

Around this time, Rita fell in love with a doctor named Leonard Gordon. Rita married Lenny in 1965, and two years later, they welcomed their daughter, Fernanda.

This was a happy time for Rita. For much of the 1970s, she starred in the PBS series *The Electric Company,* a fun educational children's show. Rita's character was known for yelling the catchphrase:

Hey, you guys!

In 1977, Rita became the first Latina and the third person ever to earn an EGOT by winning the four major entertainment awards: an Emmy, a Grammy, an Oscar, and a Tony.

She won the Emmy for her performance on *The Muppet Show*, the Grammy for *The Electric Company Album* (featuring songs Rita and the rest of the cast performed on the show), the Oscar for *West Side Story*, and the Tony for her acting in the Broadway play *The Ritz*.

Rita continued acting in a variety of TV shows for both children and adults. In 1995, when she was sixty-four years old, she received a star on the Hollywood Walk of Fame.

In 2021, director Steven Spielberg asked Rita to produce and star in a remake of *West Side Story.* This time, at age eighty-nine, she played a shopkeeper named Valentina. Rita became a mentor to Ariana DeBose, the actor who took on her original role, Anita. In 2022, sixty years after Rita won her Oscar, Ariana won the award for the same role!

Rita Moreno has lived the American dream. Her hard work and success broke barriers in Hollywood, opening doors for future generations of Latina women reaching for stardom.

¡Gracias, Rita!